Fluke was having a bad day. His tail was trembling. His heart was pounding. His thoughts were racing.

"It's no use!" cried Fluke. "I just can't do it!"

"What can't you do?" asked his mother.

"Dive to the bottom of the sea," replied Fluke.

"Diving takes lots of practice."

"Can you teach me tomorrow Mum?"

"Okay," replied his mother, "but you will have to work hard."

The next morning Fluke started his lessons.
"The secret to diving is learning how to breathe," said his mother.
Fluke laughed. "I already know how to breathe."
"Show me how deep you can dive," said his mum with a smile.
Fluke took a breath. His heart started pounding. His thoughts began racing. He tried to dive. He just couldn't do it.

"You can do it Fluke," said his mother, "but you have to relax. The real secret to diving is learning to breathe deeply."

Fluke didn't understand. "I always take a big breath before I try to dive," he explained. "Let me show you."

Fluke took a big breath. His heart started pounding. His thoughts began racing. His tail started trembling. He tried to dive. He couldn't do it.

“Fluke, you're breathing with your chest,” said his mother. “The real secret to diving is learning to breathe deeply with your belly.”

“I don't understand,” said Fluke.

Mum explained. “When you take a breath, your chest should hardly move at all - it's your belly that should expand. Your belly should inflate like a balloon. It takes lots of practice Fluke. Are you ready?”

Fluke nodded.

"Put one flipper on your chest," said his mum. "Put your other flipper on your belly. Breathe out all your air. Slowly breathe in and feel your belly rise. Now breathe out slowly letting all the air out of your balloon."

Fluke and his mother repeated their belly breathing many times.

"Let's try a dive," said his mum.

Fluke took a belly breath. His heart was pounding but not quite as hard. He was thinking about his breathing a little more. His tail trembled a little less. He tried to dive. He still couldn't do it.

“It's no use!” Fluke cried. “I can't catch my breath.”

Fluke's mother smiled. “The real secret to diving is learning to breathe deeply with your belly and staying calm. Let's try again.”

"Breathe out," said his mother. "As you breathe in and your belly rises, feel the air travel all the way to the top of your head. Slowly breathe out. Feel the air take all of your worries down to the tip of your tail."

Fluke and his mother practised this many times.

"Let's try a dive," said his mother.

Fluke thought about his breathing. His heart rate slowed down. The balloon in his belly expanded with air. As he dived, Fluke's powerful tail pushed him deeper and deeper. He didn't reach the bottom of the sea but he swam deeper than he had ever swum before.

"Almost!" yelled Fluke with excitement.

"Well done," said his mother.

Fluke smiled. "Let's try that again!"

Activities

Talk about what you think is happening in each of these pictures.

Activities

Talk about what you think is happening in each of these pictures.

Activities

Talk about what you think is happening in each of these pictures.

Activities

Talk about what you think is happening in each of these pictures.

Knowledge Books and Software
PO Box 50, Sandgate, Queensland 4017 Australia
p. +617-5568 0288 f. +617-5568 0277 email: sales@kbs.com.au

First published 2016

ISBN 9781875219308

Author: Michael Paulsen
Illustrator: Marina Savia
Layup and design: Dean Maynard
Producer: Corey White
Publisher: Rob Watts

Series information: Healthy Me! series

The Whale Who Couldn't Breathe

Fluke the baby sperm whale is having a bad day. No matter how hard he tries, he just can't dive to the bottom of the sea. Fluke turns to his mum for advice. Will she be able to help Fluke with his diving?

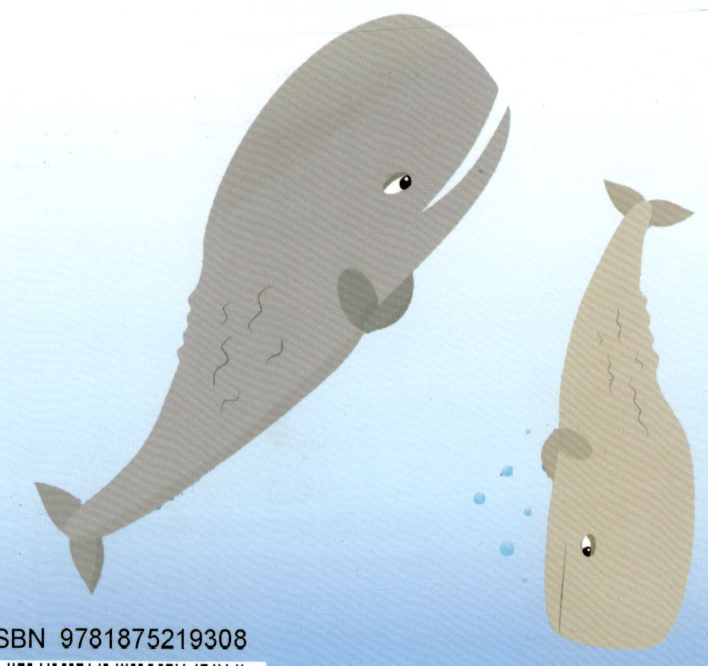

ISBN 9781875219308

Healthy Me

www.kbs.com.au